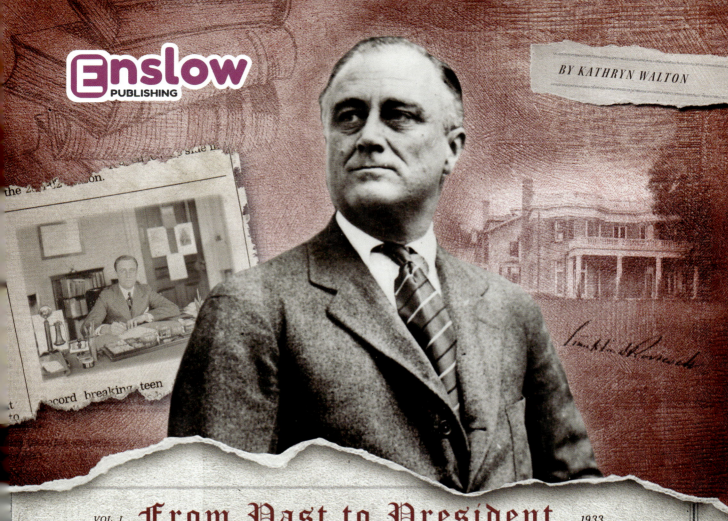

VOL. I **From Past to President** 1933

FRANKLIN D. ROOSEVELT

Enslow Publishing

BY KATHRYN WALTON

Please visit our website, www.enslow.com. For a free color catalog of all our high-quality books, call toll free 1-800-398-2504 or fax 1-877-980-4454.

Library of Congress Cataloging-in-Publication Data
Names: Walton, Kathryn, 1993- author.
Title: Franklin D. Roosevelt / Kathryn Walton.
Description: Buffalo, NY : Enslow Publishing, [2025] | Series: From past to president | Includes bibliographical references and index.
Identifiers: LCCN 2024028841 (print) | LCCN 2024028842 (ebook) | ISBN 9781978542372 (library binding) | ISBN 9781978542365 (paperback) | ISBN 9781978542389 (ebook)
Subjects: LCSH: Roosevelt, Franklin D. (Franklin Delano), 1882-1945–Juvenile literature. | Presidents–United States–Biography–Juvenile literature. | United States–Politics and government–1933-1945–Juvenile literature.
Classification: LCC E807 .W325 2025 (print) | LCC E807 (ebook) | DDC 973.917092 [B]–dc23/eng/20240723
LC record available at https://lccn.loc.gov/2024028841
LC ebook record available at https://lccn.loc.gov/2024028842

Published in 2025 by
Enslow Publishing
2544 Clinton Street
Buffalo, NY 14224

Copyright © 2025 Enslow Publishing

Portions of this work were originally authored by Gillian Gosman and published as *Franklin D. Roosevelt*. All new material in this edition is authored by Kathryn Walton.

Designer: Claire Zimmermann
Editor: Natalie Humphrey

Photo credits: Cover (Franklin D. Roosevelt portrait) Franklin_D._Roosevelt_in_Warm_Springs,_Georgia_-_NARA_-_195409.jpg/Wikimedia Commons; cover (Roosevelt's Hyde Park home), p. 17 (poster on left) Everett Collection/Shutterstock.com; cover (young Roosevelt photo) courtesy of Naval History and Heritage Command; cover (stacked books illustration) Yulistrator/Shutterstock.com; cover (newspaper clipping) STILLFX/Shutterstock.com; cover (Franklin D. Roosevelt signature) Franklin_D_Roosevelt_Signature.png/Wikimedia Commons; cover (author name scrap); series art (caption background) Robyn Mackenzie/Shutterstock.com; series art (red paper background) OLeksiiTooz/Shutterstock.com; cover (newspaper text background at lower left) MaryValery/Shutterstock.com; series art (newspaper text background) TanyaFox/Shutterstock.com; series art (More to Learn antique tag) Mega Pixel/Shutterstock.com; pp. 5, 6, 13, 17 (ripped blank newspaper piece) STILLFX/Shutterstock.com; pp. 5, 9 FDR Presidential Library & Museum/flickr; p. 6 Theodore_and_Franklin_D._Roosevelt_with_defense_attorney_W._H._Van_Benschoten.jpg/Wikimedia Commons; p. 7 NAID 196557/National Archives and Records Administration; p. 11 courtesy of the Library of Congress; p. 12 Franklin_D._Roosevelt,_Superlative_Tire_Cover.png/Wikimedia Commons; p. 13 Kheel Center/flickr; p. 15 NAID 195578/National Archives and Records Administration; p. 14 Civilian_Conservation_Corps.svg/Wikimedia Commons; p. 17 (photo on right) WPA_sign_for_paving_project_in_Opelousas_Louisiana_1938.jpg/Wikimedia Commons; p. 19 Yalta_Conference_1945_Churchill,_Stalin,_Roosevelt.jpg/Wikimedia Commons.

All rights reserved. No part of this book may be reproduced in any form without permission in writing from the publisher, except by a reviewer.

Some of the images in this book illustrate individuals who are models. The depictions do not imply actual situations or events.

Printed in the United States of America

CPSIA compliance information: Batch #CWENS25: For further information contact Enslow Publishing at 1-800-398-2504.

Find us on

CONTENTS

President Franklin D. Roosevelt 4

Young Roosevelt. 6

Entering Politics. 8

The Great Depression 10

Running for President 12

A Busy Start to Presidency 14

The New Deal's Programs 16

World War II 18

Remembering Roosevelt .20

President Roosevelt's Timeline 21

Glossary 22

For More Information 23

Index 24

Words in the glossary appear in **bold** type the first time they are used in the text.

PRESIDENT
FRANKLIN D. ROOSEVELT

Franklin Delano Roosevelt is often called one of America's greatest presidents. He led the United States through not only the Great Depression, but also part of World War II. To do this, Roosevelt had to make a lot of hard choices. But Roosevelt wasn't willing to back down from the challenge.

Roosevelt created plans, made speeches, and gave the American people hope. But before Roosevelt became president, he was a young man from Hyde Park, New York.

Franklin D. Roosevelt was the 32nd president of the United States.

MORE TO KNOW

Roosevelt was president from 1933 to 1945. This is the longest of any U.S. president in history.

YOUNG ROOSEVELT

Franklin Delano Roosevelt was born to a wealthy family on January 30, 1882. Roosevelt went to Harvard University and then Columbia Law School. Roosevelt was a good student. He passed the test to become a **lawyer** before he even finished law school!

MORE TO KNOW

Franklin Roosevelt looked up to Theodore "Teddy" Roosevelt. Franklin wanted to be a strong leader just like Teddy was.

Theodore Roosevelt

Eleanor Roosevelt

Eleanor and Franklin were **distant** cousins.

In 1905, he married Anna Eleanor Roosevelt. Eleanor was the niece of President Theodore Roosevelt. Franklin Roosevelt and Eleanor Roosevelt had six children together. Five of his children would live to be adults.

ENTERING
POLITICS

Roosevelt was interested in **politics** for much of his life. In 1910, Roosevelt was elected to the New York State Senate. In 1920, he ran as the Democratic **candidate** for U.S. vice president. He lost.

In 1921, Roosevelt caught polio. This illness left him **paralyzed** from the waist down. When he was well enough, he returned to politics. In 1928 and again in 1930, he became the governor of New York.

MORE TO KNOW

Roosevelt was 39 when he had polio. He worked hard by swimming and exercising to get some of the use of his legs back.

Roosevelt often used a wheelchair to help him get around.

THE GREAT DEPRESSION

The stock market crashed on October 29, 1929. **Investors** on Wall Street tried to trade, or sell, nearly 16 million stocks in one day. The market couldn't keep up with the sales and crashed. Many people lost their money. This was one of the causes of the Great Depression.

The Great Depression was the worst **economic** time in American history. Nearly 30 million Americans had lost their jobs by 1933. Many people lost their homes and didn't have money for food.

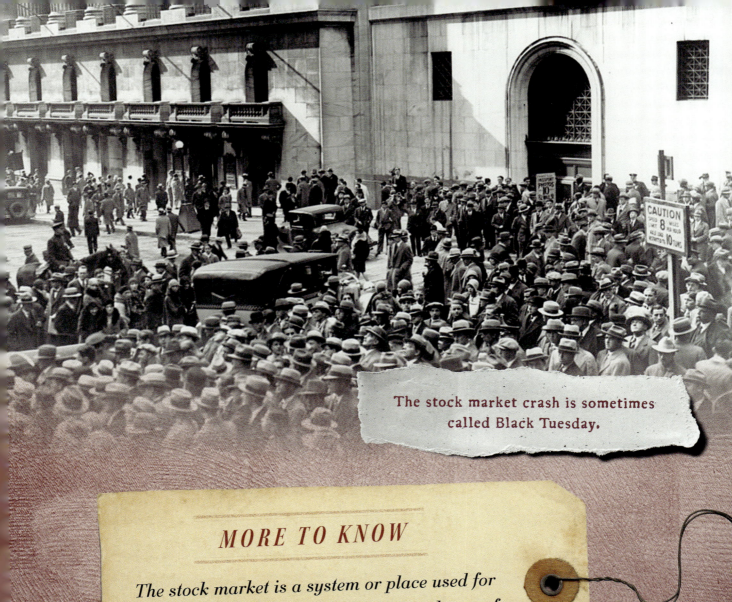

The stock market crash is sometimes called Black Tuesday.

MORE TO KNOW

The stock market is a system or place used for buying and selling stocks. Stocks are shares of a company's value that can be bought, traded, or sold as an investment.

11

RUNNING FOR PRESIDENT

By 1932, the American people needed a change. Many people blamed President Herbert Hoover for the Great Depression. A Republican president had been in office for nearly the past 12 years, and the American people wanted someone new.

Roosevelt ran as the Democratic presidential candidate in 1932. He promised to begin programs to help the country recover from the Depression. Roosevelt defeated Herbert Hoover and became president.

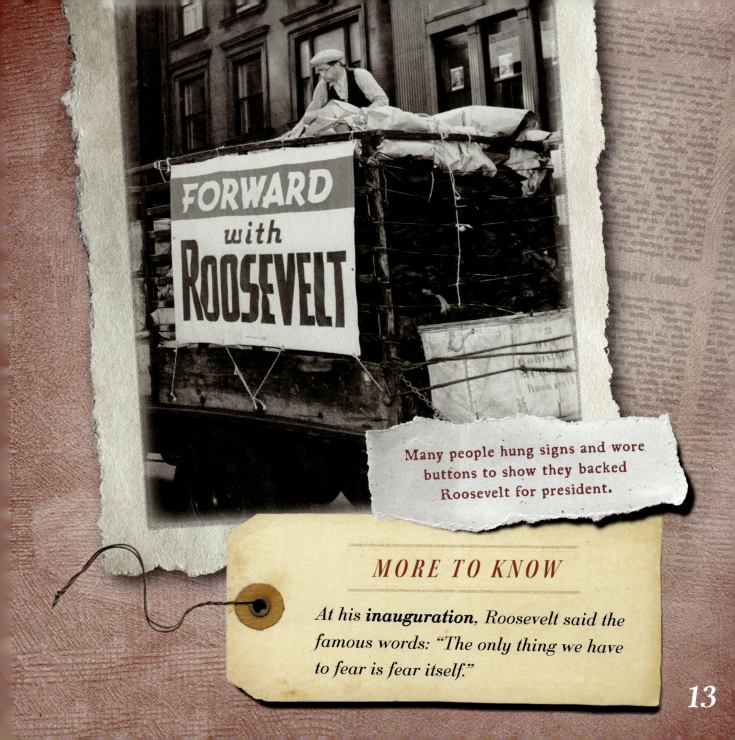

Many people hung signs and wore buttons to show they backed Roosevelt for president.

MORE TO KNOW

At his **inauguration**, Roosevelt said the famous words: "The only thing we have to fear is fear itself."

A BUSY START
TO PRESIDENCY

Roosevelt got right to work in his first 100 days as president. He started many programs that were known as the New Deal. This was because they promised Americans a fresh start.

Roosevelt started programs that gave food, housing, and work to people who needed it. He also passed laws that helped control the banking system in the United States, and an act that gave workers the right to form **unions**.

Roosevelt introduced a second New Deal in 1935 to further help people in need.

MORE TO KNOW

Roosevelt was reelected in 1936, 1940, and 1944. He is the only president to serve more than two terms in office.

THE NEW DEAL'S
PROGRAMS

The New Deal did a lot for the United States! The Tennessee Valley Authority built dams across the South. This helped stop flooding and brought electricity to many places.

The Social Security Act gave money to people who were out of work and to older Americans. The Federal Writers' Project sent writers around the country to record stories and music from people. The Civilian **Conservation** Corps gave people jobs in the national parks and forests.

MORE TO KNOW

Roosevelt also created the Works Progress Administration (WPA). This program gave work to many unemployed people including women and African Americans.

The New Deal's WPA alone helped more than 8.5 million people.

WORLD WAR II

In the beginning of 1939, Germany **invaded** Poland. This invasion started a war that spread across Europe. The German forces joined together with many other nations, including Japan and Italy, forming the Axis powers.

Roosevelt didn't want to get the United States to take part in the European war. But on December 7, 1941, the Japanese navy attacked the U.S. naval base at Pearl Harbor in Hawaii. This attack drew the United States into the war.

President Roosevelt (center) is seen here with Prime Minister of Great Britain Winston Churchill (left) and Joseph Stalin (right), a leader of the Soviet Union.

MORE TO KNOW

The United States, Great Britain, and the Soviet Union were part of the Allied powers during World War II. These three powerful countries were known as the Big Three.

19

REMEMBERING ROOSEVELT

Roosevelt led the United States through most of World War II, but he wouldn't live to see the end. While having his portrait painted in Warm Springs, Georgia, Roosevelt suffered from a **stroke**. Roosevelt died on April 12, 1945. World War II ended on September 2, 1945.

Today, many of the programs Roosevelt created are still around. While the programs may not look exactly the same, they are still helping the elderly and unemployed.

MORE TO KNOW

*The Twenty-Second **Amendment** passed in 1951. It keeps presidents from serving more than two terms.*

PRESIDENT ROOSEVELT'S TIMELINE

JANUARY 30, 1882

Franklin D. Roosevelt is born in Hyde Park, New York.

MARCH 17, 1905

He marries Anna Eleanor Roosevelt.

1910

Roosevelt is elected as a state senator in New York.

1920

He runs for vice president.

1921

Roosevelt falls ill with polio.

NOVEMBER 1932

He is elected president for the first time.

MARCH 1933

Roosevelt begins the first 100 days of his time in office and his New Deal plan.

NOVEMBER 1936

Roosevelt is reelected for the second time.

NOVEMBER 1940

He is reelected for the third time.

DECEMBER 7, 1941

The Japanese attack Pearl Harbor.

NOVEMBER 1944

Roosevelt is reelected for the fourth time.

APRIL 12, 1945

Roosevelt dies in Warm Springs, Georgia.

SEPTEMBER 2, 1945

World War II ends.

GLOSSARY

amendment: A change made to a constitution.

candidate: A person who runs in an election.

conservation: The care of the natural world.

distant: Having to do with a family member who is not closely related to another family member

economic: Having to do with the money made in an area and how it is made.

inauguration: A ceremony marking the start of one's term in public office.

invade: To enter a place to take it over.

investor: One who spends money in order to make more money in the future.

lawyer: Someone whose job it is to help people with their questions and problems with the law.

paralyzed: To be unable to move.

politics: The activities of the government and government officials.

stroke: A sudden blockage or break of a blood vessel in the brain.

union: A group of workers that join together to argue for better benefits.

FOR MORE INFORMATION

BOOKS

London, Martha. *Franklin D. Roosevelt.* Lake Elmo, MN: Focus Readers, 2023.

Pettiford, Rebecca. *Franklin D. Roosevelt.* Minneapolis, MN: Bellwether Media, 2023.

WEBSITES

Britannica Kids: Franklin D. Roosevelt
https://kids.britannica.com/kids/article/Franklin-D-Roosevelt/345521
Learn more about President Franklin D. Roosevelt's life and presidency.

National Geographic Kids: Franklin Roosevelt
kids.nationalgeographic.com/history/article/franklin-roosevelt
Find out more about Roosevelt's life before and after he became president.

Publisher's note to educators and parents: Our editors have carefully reviewed these websites to ensure that they are suitable for students. Many websites change frequently, however, and we cannot guarantee that a site's future contents will continue to meet our high standards of quality and educational value. Be advised that students should be closely supervised whenever they access the internet.

INDEX

Allied powers, 19

attack on Pearl Harbor, 18, 21

children, 7

Columbia Law School, 6

death, 20, 21

first presidential run, 12, 21

governor, 8

Great Depression, 4, 10, 12

Harvard University, 6

health, 8, 9, 21

Hyde Park, New York, 4, 21

New Deal, 14, 15, 16, 17, 21

presidential terms, 15, 20\

reelections, 15, 21

Roosevelt, Anna Eleanor, 7, 21

Roosevelt, Theodore, 6, 7

stock market crash, 10, 11

Twenty-Second Amendment, 20

World War II, 4, 18, 19, 20, 21